STEPPING OUT

MEGAN SNOW

STEPPING OUT

CONTENTS

- Stepping Out: A Guide to Mastering Independence
  1

- Structured Approach
  2

- Introduction: A Journey to Independence
  3

- Inspiration
  4

- How to Read This Book
  6

- The Importance
  7

- Practical Advice
  8

- Chapter 1: The Journey Begins
  10

- Chapter 2: Financial Literacy 101
  17

- Chapter 3: Bill Breakdown
  24

- Chapter 4: Banking Basics
  33

- Chapter 5: The Art of Saving
  40

- Chapter 6: Resume Writing
  47

- Chapter 7: The Interview Process
  51

- Chapter 8: Job Hunting
  56

- Chapter 9: Juggling Act
  76

- Chapter 10: Budgeting Blueprint
  85

- Chapter 11: Credit Creation
  95

- Chapter 12: Investment Insights
  108

- Chapter 13: Insurance Information
  113

- Chapter 14: Taking the First Step
  118

Summary
122

STEPPING OUT: A GUIDE TO MASTERING INDEPENDENCE

———————

Structured Approach

This book provides a structured approach to tackling the complexities of adulthood, with each chapter dedicated to a key aspect of living independently in a challenging economic environment. From the basics of financial literacy to the nuances of credit scores and investments, the book aims to equip young adults with the knowledge and skills necessary to thrive. Practical advice, real-world examples, and actionable steps will guide readers through the process of building a solid foundation for their adult lives. The final chapter looks to the future, encouraging continuous learning and adaptation in an ever-changing world.

INTRODUCTION: A JOURNEY TO INDEPENDENCE

When I first embarked on the journey of writing this book, I had one person in mind: my little sister. Watching her navigate the complexities of adulthood, I realized how daunting it can be for young adults starting out on their own. The world today is filled with challenges that make it almost impossible to be independent. The economy is unforgiving, and the path to self-sufficiency is fraught with obstacles. Yet, it is a journey that many of us must undertake, and it is one that can be made easier with the right guidance and tools.

My sister, like many young adults, faced the daunting task of stepping into the world with limited knowledge about managing finances, securing jobs, and maintaining her well-being all at the same time. I saw her struggle with the same issues that I had faced, and it struck me that there was a need for a comprehensive guide to help young adults navigate these challenges. This book is my attempt to provide that guidance, to offer a road map for those who are just starting out and trying to find their way.

Inspiration

Inspiration from My Little Sister
My sister has become a source of inspiration for me. Her determination, resilience, and unwavering spirit in the face of adversity have been nothing short of remarkable. Watching her grow and tackle the challenges of adulthood made me realize how important it is to have a support system and access to practical advice. I wanted to create something that could serve as that support system for her and for countless others like her.

I decided to write this book as I wanted to compile all the knowledge and experiences I had gained over the years into a single, accessible resource that could help young adults navigate the complexities of life.

The Challenges of Independence
The journey to independence is not an easy one. The world today is vastly different from what it was a few decades ago. The cost of living has skyrocketed, job markets are competitive, and the pressure to succeed is immense. For young adults, these challenges can be overwhelming. It is easy to feel lost and unsure of where to start.

One of the biggest challenges is financial independence. Managing money, understanding credit, and saving for the future are skills that are not always taught in school. Many young adults find themselves struggling with debt, living paycheck to paycheck, and unable to save for emergencies or future goals. This book aims to provide practical advice on budgeting, saving, and managing finances effectively.

Another significant challenge is finding and maintaining stable employment. The job market is constantly evolving, and the skills required to succeed are changing rapidly. Young adults need to be adaptable, continuously learning, and willing to take on new challenges. This book offers tips on job hunting, resume building, and career advancement to help young adults secure and excel in their chosen fields.

How to Read This Book

A Tool for Navigating Adulthood

This book is designed to be a tool for navigating adulthood. It is not meant to be read cover to cover in one sitting, although you certainly can if you wish. Instead, it is structured in a way that allows you to pick and choose the chapters that are most relevant to you at any given time. Whether you are looking for advice on opening a bank account, managing multiple jobs, or saving for a vacation, you can find the information you need when you need it.

Each chapter is filled with practical tips, real-life examples, and actionable advice. I have drawn from my own experiences, as well as the experiences of others, to provide a comprehensive guide that covers a wide range of topics. My goal is to make this book a valuable resource that you can turn to whenever you face a new challenge or need guidance on a particular issue.

The Importance

The Economy Today

The current economic climate is one of the biggest hurdles for young adults striving for independence. The cost of living continues to rise, wages have not kept pace with inflation, and the job market is increasingly competitive. It is more important than ever to be financially savvy and to make informed decisions about your money.

This book provides strategies for managing your finances in a challenging economy. From creating a budget to understanding investments, you will find the tools you need to make smart financial decisions. I also discuss the importance of building an emergency fund, planning for retirement, and avoiding common financial pitfalls.

Practical Advice

Practical Advice for Real-Life Situations

One of the key features of this book is its focus on practical advice for real-life situations. I have included tips and strategies that you can implement immediately to improve your financial situation, enhance your career prospects, and maintain your well-being. Here are a few examples of what you will find in this book:

- Budgeting: Learn how to create a budget that works for you, track your expenses, and stick to your financial goals.
- Saving for a Vacation: Discover strategies for saving money on a limited income and planning a budget-friendly vacation.
- Managing Multiple Jobs: Get tips on how to juggle multiple jobs, stay organized, and avoid burnout.
- Building Credit: Understand the importance of credit, how to build a good credit score, and how to avoid debt.
- Career Advancement: Find out how to set career goals, seek promotions, and continuously improve your skills.

A Message of Encouragement

Writing this book has been a labor of love. It is my hope that it will serve as a valuable resource for young adults who are just starting out on their journey to independence.

I want you to know that you are not alone in this journey. There are countless others who have faced the same challenges and have found ways to overcome them.

Remember, the path to independence is not a straight line. There will be ups and downs, successes and setbacks, but with determination, resilience, and the right tools, you can achieve your goals and build a fulfilling and independent life.

Thank you for choosing to read this book. I hope that the information and advice contained within these pages will help you navigate the complexities of adulthood and achieve your dreams. Whether you read it cover to cover or pick the chapters that apply to you at a certain time, I encourage you to use this book as a tool to guide you on your journey.

Good luck on your journey to independence. Remember, you have the power to shape your future and achieve your goals. Stay focused, stay motivated, and never stop learning. You have the potential to succeed and get ahead in life, and I am here to support you every step of the way.

Thank You and Good Luck!

CHAPTER 1: THE JOURNEY BEGINS

As I stood in my childhood bedroom, surrounded by boxes and memories, I felt a mix of emotions swirling inside me. Excitement for the future, fear of the unknown, and a hint of sadness for leaving behind the comfort and security of my family's home. I was finally taking the leap into adulthood, and it felt both exhilarating and terrifying.

I had just graduated from college, and my parents had graciously allowed me to stay at home for a few months while I got my bearings. But now, it was time to spread my wings and fly. I had found a small apartment in the city, secured a job in my field, and was ready to start building a life of my own.

As I looked around my room, I realized that this was more than just a physical move. This was a symbolic transition from dependence to independence. I was leaving behind the safety net of my family's support and venturing into the unknown.

I took a deep breath, shouldered my backpack, and headed out the door. My parents hugged me tightly, tears in their eyes. "We're so proud of you," they said. "You're ready for this."

I nodded, trying to convince myself as much as them.

The first few weeks of independence were a whirlwind of excitement and adjustment. I explored my new neighborhood, tried new restaurants, and made new friends. I felt like I was on top of the world.

But as the days turned into weeks, reality began to set in. Bills piled up, and my bank account dwindled. I struggled to balance work and play, often finding myself working late into the night and sleeping in until noon.

I began to wonder if I was truly cut out for this whole adulthood thing.

One day, as I was scrubbing last night's dishes, I felt a wave of doubt wash over me. What was I doing? I was barely scraping by, and I had no idea how to adult.

But then I remembered why I had taken this leap in the first place. I wanted to be independent, to forge my own path, and to build a life that was truly mine.

I took a deep breath, wiped away my tears, and kept scrubbing.

As the months went by, I slowly found my footing. I learned to budget, to cook, and to prioritize. I discovered that adulthood wasn't about having all the answers; it was about figuring things out as I went.

And with each passing day, I felt myself growing more confident, more self-assured. I was doing this. I was actually doing this.

Starting off adulthood as a young adult trying to be independent is a journey, not a destination. It's a journey of trial and error, of growth and exploration. And it's okay to stumble, to falter, and to make mistakes.

Because in the end, it's not about being perfect; it's about being brave enough to take the leap.

The First Steps

The first few days in my new apartment were a blur of unpacking and organizing. I had never realized how much stuff I had accumulated over the years. Each item I pulled out of a box brought back a flood of memories. There was the old teddy bear that had been my constant companion during childhood, the high school yearbooks filled with messages from friends, and the college textbooks that had seen me through countless all-nighters.

Setting up my new space was both exciting and overwhelming. I wanted everything to be perfect, but I quickly realized that perfection was an unrealistic goal. My apartment was small, and I had to make do with what I had. I learned to appreciate the charm of my mismatched furniture and the coziness of my tiny kitchen.

One of the first challenges I faced was cooking for myself. Growing up, my mom had always prepared delicious meals, and I had taken her culinary skills for granted. Now, I was on my own, armed with a few basic recipes and a lot of enthusiasm. My first attempts at cooking were far from perfect. I burned the toast, overcooked the pasta, and managed to set off the smoke alarm more than once. But with each meal, I got a little better. I learned to enjoy the process of experimenting in the kitchen and discovered a newfound appreciation for home-cooked food.

Building a Routine

As the days turned into weeks, I began to establish a routine. I woke up early, went for a jog in the nearby park, and then headed to work. My job was demanding, but I found it fulfilling. I was learning new skills, meeting interesting people, and contributing to projects that I was passionate about. The sense of accomplishment I felt at the end of each day was a reward in itself.

Balancing work and personal life was a challenge. There were days when I felt overwhelmed by the demands of my job and the responsibilities of maintaining my apartment. However,f I learned to prioritize and manage my time effectively. I set aside time for self-care, whether it was reading a book, taking a long bath, or simply relaxing with a cup of tea. These moments of solitude helped me recharge and stay focused.

Financial Independence

One of the most significant aspects of adulthood was managing my finances. For the first time, I was responsible for paying rent, utilities, and other bills. I had to budget my income and make sure I was saving for the future. It was a steep learning curve, but I embraced the challenge. I created a spreadsheet to track my expenses and set financial goals for myself. I learned to distinguish between needs and wants and made conscious decisions about my spending.

There were times when I had to make sacrifices. I couldn't afford to eat out as often as I wanted, and I had to resist the temptation to splurge on unnecessary items. But these sacrifices were worth it. I felt a sense of pride in being able to support myself and make responsible financial choices.

The Importance of Community

Living on my own didn't mean I was alone. I made an effort to build a sense of community in my new neighborhood. I introduced myself to my neighbors, attended local events, and joined clubs and organizations that aligned with my interests. These connections provided a support system and made me feel more at home.

I also stayed in touch with my family and friends. Regular phone calls, video chats, and visits helped bridge the distance and kept our relationships strong. I realized that independence didn't mean isolating myself; it meant finding a balance between self-reliance and staying connected with loved ones.

Overcoming Challenges

Adulthood came with its fair share of challenges. There were moments of doubt, frustration, and loneliness. I faced setbacks at work, dealt with unexpected expenses, and navigated the complexities of adult relationships. But each challenge was an opportunity for growth. I learned to be resilient, to adapt to changing circumstances, and to find solutions to problems.

One of the most valuable lessons I learned was the importance of asking for help. There were times when I felt overwhelmed and didn't know how to proceed. In those moments, I reached out to my parents, mentors, and friends for guidance. Their support and advice were invaluable, and I realized that seeking help was a sign of strength, not weakness.

Embracing Change

As I settled into my new life, I began to embrace change. I understood that adulthood was a continuous journey of self-discovery and growth. I set new goals for myself, both personally and professionally. I pursued hobbies and interests that brought me joy and fulfillment. I took risks and stepped out of my comfort zone, knowing that each experience would shape me into the person I was meant to be.

Reflection and Gratitude

Looking back on my journey, I felt a deep sense of gratitude. I was grateful for the support of my family, the opportunities I had been given, and the lessons I had learned along the way. I realized that adulthood was not about having all the answers but about being open to learning and growing.

I also recognized the importance of self-compassion. There were times when I made mistakes or fell short of my expectations. But instead of being overly critical, I learned to be kind to myself. I acknowledged my efforts and celebrated my achievements, no matter how small.

Moving Forward

As I continued on my journey, I felt a sense of excitement for the future. I knew that there would be more challenges and uncertainties ahead, but I was ready to face them with confidence and resilience. I had built a strong foundation for myself, and I was determined to keep growing and evolving.

Adulthood was not a destination but a continuous journey. It was a journey of self-discovery, growth, and exploration. It was about embracing change, overcoming challenges, and finding joy in the little moments. And most importantly, it was about being brave enough to take the leap and trust in my ability to navigate the path ahead.

CHAPTER 2: FINANCIAL LITERACY 101

As I stepped into adulthood, I was hit with a harsh reality – I knew nothing about managing my finances. My parents had always handled the money, and I had never paid attention. But now, with a steady income and bills to pay, I was forced to confront my financial ignorance.

At first, I tried to wing it, relying on intuition and guesswork. But as the months went by, I found myself drowning in debt, struggling to make ends meet, and feeling overwhelmed by the complexity of it all. That's when I realized that financial literacy wasn't just about knowing how to balance a checkbook or create a budget – it was about understanding the psychology of money, the emotional triggers that drove my spending habits, and the long-term implications of my financial decisions.

The Wake-Up Call

The first wake-up call came when I received my first credit card bill. I had been swiping my card without a second thought, assuming that my future self would handle the payments. But when I saw the total amount due, I felt a wave of panic. How had I spent so much? And more importantly, how was I going to pay it off?

I realized that I needed to take control of my finances, and fast. The first step was to understand where my money was going. I started by tracking my expenses, categorizing my spending, and identifying areas where I could cut back. This was an eye-opening exercise. I discovered that I was spending a significant portion of my income on dining out, entertainment, and impulse purchases.

The 50/30/20 Rule

One of the most valuable lessons I learned was the 50/30/20 rule. This simple budgeting guideline suggests allocating 50% of your income towards necessities (like rent, utilities, and groceries), 30% towards discretionary spending (like dining out, hobbies, and entertainment), and 20% towards saving and debt repayment. This rule helped me create a balanced budget that allowed me to cover my essential expenses while still enjoying some of life's pleasures.

Understanding the Psychology of Money

But financial literacy is not just about numbers; it's also about understanding the psychology of money. I had to confront my own biases and assumptions about money and develop a healthy relationship with it. I realized that my spending habits were often driven by emotional triggers. For example, I tended to splurge on shopping when I was feeling stressed or unhappy. Recognizing these patterns helped me make more mindful spending decisions.

Building an Emergency Fund

One of the first financial goals I set for myself was to build an emergency fund. An emergency fund is a savings account that you can tap into in case of unexpected expenses, like medical bills or car repairs. Financial experts recommend having at least three to six months' worth of living expenses saved up. This may seem like a daunting goal, but I started small, setting aside a portion of each paycheck until I reached my target.

Saving for Retirement

Another important aspect of financial literacy is saving for retirement. When you're young, retirement may seem like a distant concern, but the earlier you start saving, the better off you'll be. I learned about the power of compound interest, which allows your savings to grow exponentially over time. I opened a retirement account and started contributing a percentage of my income each month. Even small contributions can add up significantly over the years.

Investing Wisely

Investing is another key component of financial literacy. I used to think that investing was only for the wealthy or for those with a deep understanding of the stock market. But I soon realized that anyone can invest, and it's an essential part of building wealth. I started by educating myself about different types of investments, such as stocks, bonds, and mutual funds. I also learned about the importance of diversification, which involves spreading your investments across different asset classes to reduce risk.

Avoiding High-Interest Debt

One of the biggest financial pitfalls to avoid is high-interest debt. Credit card debt, in particular, can quickly spiral out of control if you're not careful. I made it a priority to pay off my credit card balance in full each month to avoid interest charges. If you already have high-interest debt, consider consolidating it with a lower-interest loan or balance transfer credit card to make it more manageable.

Continuous Education

Financial literacy is a journey, not a destination. It requires patience, discipline, and self-awareness. I made a commitment to continuously educate myself about personal finance. I read books, attended workshops, and followed financial experts online. Staying informed helped me adapt to changing circumstances and make informed financial decisions.

Setting Financial Goals

Setting financial goals is crucial for staying motivated and on track. I created both short-term and long-term goals for myself. Short-term goals included things like paying off my credit card debt and building my emergency fund. Long-term goals included saving for a down payment on a house and planning for retirement. Having clear goals gave me a sense of purpose and direction.

The Importance of Patience and Discipline

Achieving financial literacy requires patience and discipline. There were times when I felt like giving up, especially when faced with setbacks and challenges. But I persevered, driven by a growing sense of financial confidence and independence. I began to see the world in a different light - as a place of opportunity and possibility, rather than scarcity and limitation.

Financial Literacy as a Societal Issue

As I looked around, I realized that I was not alone. Many of my peers were struggling with the same issues - debt, financial insecurity, and a lack of financial knowledge. That's when I knew that financial literacy was not just a personal issue - it was a societal one. It was a matter of economic justice, equality, and empowerment.

Empowering the Next Generation

As young adults, we have the power to create a different future - one where financial literacy is the norm, not the exception. One where we can make informed decisions, avoid financial pitfalls, and build a secure financial future. I started sharing my knowledge with friends and family, encouraging them to take control of their finances and educate themselves about money management.

Practical Tips for Financial Success

Here are some practical tips that I wish I had known when I first started my financial journey:

1. Create a Budget: Track your income and expenses to understand where your money is going. Use the 50/30/20 rule as a guideline.
2. Build an Emergency Fund: Aim to save three to six months' worth of living expenses for unexpected emergencies.
3. Pay Off High-Interest Debt: Focus on paying off credit card debt and other high-interest loans as quickly as possible.
4. Save for Retirement: Start contributing to a retirement account as early as possible to take advantage of compound interest.
5. Invest Wisely: Educate yourself about different types of investments and diversify your portfolio to reduce risk.
6. Live Below Your Means: Avoid lifestyle inflation and resist the temptation to spend more as your income increases.
7. Stay Informed: Continuously educate yourself about personal finance through books, workshops, and online resources.
8. Set Financial Goals: Create both short-term and long-term financial goals to stay motivated and focused.
9. Seek Professional Advice: Consider consulting a financial advisor for personalized guidance and advice.
10. Be Patient and Persistent: Financial success takes time and effort. Stay disciplined and don't give up, even when faced with challenges.

The Payoff

The journey to financial literacy is not easy, but it is worth it. It requires effort, dedication, and resilience. But the payoff is immense – financial freedom, peace of mind, and the ability to live life on our own terms. By taking control of our finances, we can create a brighter financial future – one that is secure, stable, and full of possibility.

Final Thoughts

As I reflect on my journey to financial literacy, I am grateful for the lessons I have learned and the progress I have made. I am no longer overwhelmed by the complexity of managing my finances. Instead, I feel empowered and confident in my ability to make informed financial decisions.

Financial literacy is a lifelong journey, and there is always more to learn. But by taking the first step and committing to continuous education, we can build a solid foundation for financial success. Let's awaken to the importance of financial literacy and start building a brighter financial future today.

CHAPTER 3: BILL BREAKDOWN

As I settled into my new apartment, I was faced with a daunting task: managing my monthly expenses. I had never paid bills before, and the thought of juggling rent, utilities, groceries, and other expenses was overwhelming.

But I knew I had to take control of my finances if I wanted to achieve independence. So, I sat down and made a list of all my monthly expenses.

Identifying Essential Expenses

First, there were the essentials:

- Rent: This was my largest expense and a non-negotiable part of my budget. Finding an affordable place that met my needs was crucial.
- Utilities: Electricity, water, gas, and internet were necessary for daily living. I learned to be mindful of my usage to keep these costs manageable.
- Groceries: Food is a basic necessity, but I quickly realized that meal planning and smart shopping could significantly reduce my grocery bill.
- Transportation: Whether it was a car payment, insurance, gas, or public transportation costs, getting around was essential for work and daily activities.
- Minimum Payments on Debts: Credit cards and student loans required regular payments to avoid penalties and interest accumulation.

Adding Non-Essential Expenses

Next, I added the non-essentials:

- Entertainment: Dining out, movies, and hobbies were important for my mental health and social life, but they needed to be balanced with my financial goals.
- Subscription Services: Streaming platforms and gym memberships added value to my life but required careful consideration to avoid overspending.
- Savings Goals: Building an emergency fund and saving for retirement were crucial for long-term financial security.

Categorizing and Prioritizing

I then categorized my expenses into needs and wants, and prioritized them accordingly. This helped me understand where I could cut back if necessary and where I needed to focus my financial efforts.

Paying Bills

One of the first steps I took was setting up automatic payments for all my bills. This ensured I never missed a payment and avoided late fees. I also took advantage of paperless billing and online payment options to reduce clutter and save time.

Managing Expenses

To manage my expenses, I implemented the 50/30/20 rule:

- 50% of my income went towards necessities: Rent, utilities, and groceries were my top priorities.
- 30% towards discretionary spending: Entertainment and hobbies were important, but I kept them within a reasonable budget.
- 20% towards saving and debt repayment: Building my emergency fund and paying off debts were crucial for financial stability.

The Envelope System

I also used the envelope system to track my spending. I divided my expenses into categories (groceries, entertainment, etc.) and placed the corresponding budgeted amount into an envelope for each category. This visual method helped me stay within my budget and avoid overspending.

Refining the System

As the months went by, I refined my system, making adjustments as needed. I learned to anticipate expenses, like car maintenance and property taxes, and budgeted accordingly. This proactive approach helped me avoid financial surprises and stay on track with my goals.

Tips for Managing Monthly Expenses

Here are some tips that helped me manage my monthly expenses effectively:

1. Track Your Spending: Understanding where your money is going is the first step to taking control of your finances.
2. Prioritize Needs Over Wants: Focus on essential expenses first and allocate funds to non-essentials only if your budget allows.
3. Use Automatic Payments and Paperless Billing: These tools help you stay organized and avoid late fees.
4. Implement the 50/30/20 Rule: This simple guideline helps you balance necessities, discretionary spending, and savings.
5. Use the Envelope System: This method helps you visualize your budget and stay within your spending limits.

6. Anticipate Expenses: Plan for irregular expenses, like car maintenance and property taxes, to avoid financial surprises.

Understanding Utility Bills

Utility bills can be a significant part of your monthly expenses, and understanding them is crucial for effective budgeting. Here's a breakdown of common utility bills and tips for managing them:

- Electricity: Your electricity bill can vary based on your usage. Simple habits like turning off lights when not in use, using energy-efficient appliances, and unplugging devices can help reduce your bill.
- Water: Water usage can add up quickly. Fixing leaks, taking shorter showers, and using water-saving fixtures can help lower your water bill.
- Gas: If you use gas for heating or cooking, be mindful of your usage. Regular maintenance of your heating system and using energy-efficient appliances can help reduce costs.
- Internet: Shop around for the best internet deals and consider bundling services to save money. Make sure you're not paying for more speed than you need.

Grocery Shopping on a Budget

Groceries are a necessity, but there are ways to shop smart and save money:

- Meal Planning: Plan your meals for the week and make a shopping list. This helps you avoid impulse purchases and reduces food waste.
- Buy in Bulk: Purchasing non-perishable items in bulk can save money in the long run.
- Use Coupons and Discounts: Take advantage of coupons, loyalty programs, and sales to save on groceries.
- Cook at Home: Eating out can be expensive. Cooking at home is not only cheaper but also healthier.

Transportation Costs

Transportation is another significant expense. Here are some tips to manage these costs:

- Public Transportation: If available, public transportation can be a cost-effective alternative to owning a car.
- Carpooling: Sharing rides with coworkers or friends can save on gas and reduce wear and tear on your vehicle.
- Maintenance: Regular maintenance of your car can prevent costly repairs down the line. Keep up with oil changes, tire rotations, and other routine services.
- Insurance: Shop around for the best insurance rates and consider raising your deductible to lower your premium.

Managing Debt

Debt can be overwhelming, but managing it effectively is crucial for financial stability:

- Prioritize High-Interest Debt: Focus on paying off high-interest debt, like credit cards, first. This will save you money on interest in the long run.
- Consolidate Debt: If you have multiple debts, consider consolidating them into a single loan with a lower interest rate.
- Make Extra Payments: Whenever possible, make extra payments towards your debt to pay it off faster.
- Avoid New Debt: Be cautious about taking on new debt. Only borrow what you can afford to repay.

Building Savings

Saving money is essential for financial security. Here are some strategies to build your savings:

- Automate Savings: Set up automatic transfers to your savings account. This ensures you save a portion of your income each month.
- Emergency Fund: Aim to save three to six months' worth of living expenses in an emergency fund. This provides a financial cushion in case of unexpected expenses.
- Retirement Savings: Start saving for retirement as early as possible. Take advantage of employer-sponsored retirement plans and contribute regularly.

- Set Savings Goals: Having specific savings goals, like a vacation or a down payment on a house, can motivate you to save more.

Adapting to Changing Circumstances

Life is unpredictable, and your financial situation can change. It's important to be flexible and adapt to new circumstances:

- Reevaluate Your Budget: Regularly review your budget and make adjustments as needed. This helps you stay on track with your financial goals.
- Plan for Irregular Expenses: Anticipate expenses like car repairs, medical bills, and property taxes. Set aside money each month to cover these costs.
- Stay Informed: Keep up with changes in the economy, job market, and financial regulations. Staying informed helps you make better financial decisions.

Conclusion

Navigating monthly expenses is a crucial aspect of starting off on your own. By understanding your expenses, prioritizing needs over wants, and implementing a management system, you can take control of your finances and achieve independence. Remember, managing expenses is a continuous process, and it's essential to be flexible and adapt to changing circumstances.

Taking control of your monthly expenses is a key step towards financial independence. By understanding your expenses, prioritizing needs over wants, and implementing effective management strategies, you can achieve financial stability and peace of mind. Remember, managing expenses is a continuous process, and it's essential to be flexible and adapt to changing circumstances. With patience, discipline, and a proactive approach, you can navigate the complexities of monthly expenses and build a secure financial future.

CHAPTER 4: BANKING BASICS

Introduction

Opening a bank account is a significant step towards financial independence. Whether you're just starting out or looking to better manage your finances, understanding the options available and how to use them effectively is crucial. In this chapter, we'll explore the process of opening a bank account, compare banks and credit unions, and delve into the benefits of choosing a credit union. We'll also discuss how to use different types of accounts to manage your money for various needs such as bills, entertainment, vacations, and emergency savings.

Section 1: How to Open a Bank Account

Opening a bank account is a straightforward process, but it requires some preparation. Here are the steps to get started:

1. Choose the Right Financial Institution: Decide whether you want to open an account with a bank or a credit union. We'll discuss the differences and benefits of each in the next section.
2. Gather Necessary Documents: You'll need identification (such as a driver's license or passport), proof of address (like a utility bill), and your Social Security number.
3. Complete the Application: You can usually apply online or in person. Fill out the application form with your personal information.
4. Make an Initial Deposit: Some accounts require a minimum deposit to open. Check the requirements of your chosen institution.
5. Set Up Online Banking: Most financial institutions offer online banking services. Set up your online account to manage your finances conveniently.

Section 2: Bank vs. Credit Union

When choosing where to open your account, it's essential to understand the differences between banks and credit unions.

Banks:

- For-Profit Institutions: Banks are for-profit institutions that offer a wide range of financial services.
- Accessibility: Banks often have more branches and ATMs, making them more accessible.
- Services: They provide various services, including loans, credit cards, and investment options.
- Fees: Banks may have higher fees and lower interest rates on savings accounts compared to credit unions.

Credit Unions:

- Not-for-Profit Institutions: Credit unions are member-owned and operate as not-for-profit organizations.
- Member Focused: They often provide better customer service and personalized attention.
- Lower Fees: Credit unions typically have lower fees and offer higher interest rates on savings accounts.
- Community-Oriented: They focus on serving their members and the local community.

Section 3: Benefits of Choosing a Credit Union

Choosing a credit union can offer several advantages over traditional banks:

1. Lower Fees: Credit unions generally have lower fees for services such as checking accounts, overdrafts, and ATM usage.

2. Higher Interest Rates: They often provide higher interest rates on savings accounts and certificates of deposit (CDs).
3. Personalized Service: Credit unions are known for their excellent customer service and personalized attention to members' needs.
4. Community Focus: They reinvest profits back into the community and offer financial education programs.
5. Member Ownership: As a member, you have a say in how the credit union is run, including voting on important decisions.

Section 4: Using Accounts to Manage Money

Once you've chosen a credit union and opened your accounts, it's essential to use them effectively to manage your finances. Here's how you can use different types of accounts for various needs:

1. Savings Account:

- Purpose: Use your savings account for emergency funds and long-term savings goals.
- Benefits: Higher interest rates help your money grow over time.
- Strategy: Set up automatic transfers from your checking account to your savings account to build your savings consistently.

2. Checking Account:

- Purpose: Use your checking account for everyday expenses and bill payments.
- Benefits: Easy access to your money through debit cards, checks, and online banking.
- Strategy: Keep track of your spending and maintain a buffer to avoid overdraft fees.

3. Money Market Account:

- Purpose: Use a money market account for medium-term savings goals, such as vacations or large purchases.
- Benefits: Higher interest rates than regular savings accounts and limited check-writing capabilities.
- Strategy: Use this account to save for specific goals that you plan to achieve within a few years.

4. Additional Accounts for Specific Needs:

- Bills Account: Open a separate checking account dedicated to paying bills. This helps you keep track of your monthly expenses and ensures you have enough funds to cover them.
- Entertainment Account: Use a separate account for discretionary spending on entertainment, dining out, and hobbies. This helps you manage your fun money without affecting your essential expenses.
- Vacation Account: Save for vacations by opening a dedicated savings or money market account. Set

aside a portion of your income regularly to fund your travel plans.
- Emergency Savings Account: Maintain a separate savings account for emergencies. Aim to save three to six months' worth of living expenses to cover unexpected situations.

Section 5: Setting Up and Managing Your Accounts

To make the most of your accounts, follow these steps:

1. Automate Your Finances: Set up automatic transfers and bill payments to ensure you stay on track with your financial goals.
2. Monitor Your Accounts: Regularly check your account balances and transactions to avoid overdrafts and identify any unauthorized activity.
3. Review Your Budget: Periodically review your budget and adjust your spending and saving strategies as needed.
4. Take Advantage of Online Tools: Use online banking tools and mobile apps to manage your accounts, track your spending, and set financial goals.
5. Seek Financial Advice: If you're unsure about managing your finances, consider seeking advice from a financial advisor or attending financial education workshops offered by your credit union.

Conclusion

Choosing the right financial institution and using your accounts effectively are crucial steps towards achieving financial independence. By opting for a credit union, you can benefit from lower fees, higher interest rates, and personalized service. Using different types of accounts for specific needs, such as bills, entertainment, vacations, and emergency savings, can help you manage your money more efficiently and achieve your financial goals. Remember, the key to financial success is staying organized, monitoring your accounts, and continuously educating yourself about personal finance.

CHAPTER 5: THE ART OF SAVING

Introduction

Starting out as a young adult can be challenging, especially when you're juggling college, bills, and trying to save money on a limited income. However, with the right strategies and mindset, it's possible to manage your finances effectively and build a solid foundation for your future. In this chapter, we'll explore proven strategies for saving money, best practices for financial management, and practical examples to help you navigate this crucial phase of your life.

Section 1: Understanding Your Financial Situation

Before you can start saving money, it's essential to have a clear understanding of your financial situation. This involves assessing your income, expenses, and financial goals.

1. Track Your Income and Expenses: Begin by tracking all sources of income, including part-time jobs, scholarships, and financial aid. Next, list all your expenses, such as tuition, rent, utilities, groceries, transportation, and entertainment. Use a budgeting app or a simple spreadsheet to keep everything organized.
2. Identify Your Financial Goals: Determine what you want to achieve financially. This could include saving for an emergency fund, paying off student loans, or setting aside money for future investments. Having clear goals will help you stay motivated and focused.
3. Create a Budget: Based on your income and expenses, create a realistic budget that allocates funds for essential expenses, savings, and discretionary spending. Stick to your budget as closely as possible to avoid overspending.

Section 2: Proven Strategies for Saving Money

Saving money on a limited income requires creativity and discipline. Here are some proven strategies to help you save effectively:

STEPPING OUT

1. Cut Unnecessary Expenses: Review your spending habits and identify areas where you can cut back. This might include dining out less frequently, canceling unused subscriptions, or finding more affordable alternatives for entertainment.
2. Take Advantage of Student Discounts: Many businesses offer discounts to students. Always carry your student ID and ask about discounts when shopping, dining, or using services.
3. Cook at Home: Eating out can be expensive. Save money by cooking meals at home and packing lunches for school or work. Plan your meals in advance and buy groceries in bulk to reduce costs.
4. Use Public Transportation: If you live in an area with reliable public transportation, use it instead of owning a car. This can save you money on gas, insurance, and maintenance.
5. Buy Used or Second-Hand Items: Consider buying used textbooks, clothing, and furniture. Thrift stores, online marketplaces, and campus swap events can be great places to find affordable items.
6. Limit Credit Card Use: Avoid relying on credit cards for everyday expenses. High-interest rates can lead to debt accumulation. Use credit cards responsibly and pay off the balance in full each month.
7. Find Part-Time Work: Look for part-time jobs or freelance opportunities that fit your schedule. Even a few extra hours of work each week can provide additional income to cover expenses and save.

Section 3: Best Practices for Financial Management

Effective financial management involves more than just saving money. Here are some best practices to help you manage your finances wisely:

1. Build an Emergency Fund: Aim to save at least three to six months' worth of living expenses in an emergency fund. This will provide a financial cushion in case of unexpected expenses or income loss.
2. Automate Savings: Set up automatic transfers from your checking account to your savings account. This ensures that a portion of your income is saved regularly without requiring conscious effort.
3. Pay Off High-Interest Debt: If you have high-interest debt, such as credit card balances, prioritize paying it off as quickly as possible. This will save you money on interest payments in the long run.
4. Use Financial Aid Wisely: If you're receiving financial aid, use it primarily for educational expenses. Avoid using student loans for non-essential purchases, as this can lead to higher debt after graduation.
5. Take Advantage of Campus Resources: Many colleges offer free or low-cost resources, such as career counseling, health services, and recreational facilities. Utilize these resources to save money and enhance your college experience.
6. Invest in Your Education: While saving money is important, investing in your education can lead to higher earning potential in the future. Focus on your

studies and seek opportunities for internships and networking to enhance your career prospects.

Section 4: Practical Examples and Personal Advice

To provide practical insights, let's explore some examples and personal advice on saving money as a young adult:

Example 1: Meal Planning and Grocery

- Shopping:Strategy: Plan your meals for the week and create a shopping list based on your meal plan. Stick to the list to avoid impulse purchases.
- Personal Advice: I found that meal planning not only saved me money but also reduced food waste. I would cook in bulk and freeze portions for later, which made it easier to stick to my budget.

Example 2: Utilizing Campus Resources:

- Strategy: Take advantage of free campus resources, such as the library, gym, and student events. These resources can help you save money on books, fitness memberships, and entertainment.
- Personal Advice: I wish I had used these resources during my college years, regularly using the campus gym and attending free workshops and events. This would have allowed me to stay active and engaged without spending extra money.

Example 3: Finding Affordable Housing:

- Strategy: Look for affordable housing options, such as shared apartments or dormitories. Consider living with roommates to split rent and utility costs.
- Personal Advice: I chose to live with roommates during college for a bit and also lived on my own. It was a little cheaper to live with roommates as you are splitting rent, but it did cause some headaches as we were not always on the same page and definitely not on the same schedules, so be careful if you choose to find a roommate.

Example 4: Part-Time Work and Freelancing:

- Strategy: Seek part-time jobs or freelance opportunities that align with your skills and schedule. Use the extra income to cover expenses and save.
- Personal Advice: I worked part-time in retail and also started doing some woodworking on my own. This not only provided additional income but also helped me develop valuable skills and build my resume.

Example 5: Budgeting and Tracking Expenses:

- Strategy: Create a detailed budget and track your expenses regularly. Use budgeting apps or spreadsheets to monitor your spending and identify areas for improvement.
- Personal Advice: Keeping a budget was crucial for me to stay on track with my financial goals. I re-

viewed my expenses weekly and adjusted my spending habits as needed to ensure I was saving enough. Using a planner is the best thing I have ever done! You can get them in a book format or through apps. If used right, they will help you stay organized and never miss anything!

Conclusion

Saving money as a young adult, especially when balancing bills and college, requires discipline, creativity, and a proactive approach. By understanding your financial situation, implementing proven strategies, and following best practices, you can build a strong financial foundation for your future. Remember, every small step you take towards saving and managing your money effectively will pay off in the long run. Stay focused, stay motivated, and continue to educate yourself about personal finance to achieve your financial goals.

CHAPTER 6: RESUME WRITING

Crafting Your Resume

Your resume is your personal marketing tool, a document that presents your skills, experiences, and qualifications to potential employers. Here's how to craft an effective one:

<u>Contact Information:</u> Include your full name, phone number, email address, and LinkedIn profile if you have one. Ensure your email address is professional.

<u>Objective Statement</u>: This is a brief statement about your career goals and how the job aligns with them. Tailor it to each job application.

Skills: List your relevant skills. These could be technical skills (like proficiency in a programming language) or soft skills (like communication or leadership).

Experience: Detail your work history, starting with your most recent job. Include your job title, the company's name, the dates you worked there, and bullet points highlighting your responsibilities and achievements.

Education: List your educational background, starting with the highest level of education. Include the name of the institution, the degree obtained, and the dates attended.

References: While not always necessary, having a section for references can be beneficial. Always ask for permission before listing someone as a reference.

Searching for a Good Paying Job

Finding a good paying job requires research, networking, and persistence. Here are some strategies:

Job Boards: Websites like Indeed, Glassdoor, and LinkedIn are great resources. They allow you to filter jobs by location, salary range, and more.

Networking: Attend industry events, join professional organizations, and connect with alumni from your school. Networking can often lead to job opportunities.

Company Websites: If you're interested in a specific company, check their website regularly for job postings.

Recruiters: Consider working with a recruiter. They can help match you with jobs that fit your skills and career goals.

Accepting Less Desirable Jobs

While in college or in need of extra money, it's okay to accept jobs that may not align with your career goals. These jobs can provide income, work experience, and potentially valuable connections. Remember, every job can offer something valuable, whether it's a new skill, an interesting perspective, or a stepping stone to your next opportunity.

Being an Excellent Employee

Being an excellent employee goes beyond just doing your job well. Here are some tips:

<u>Positive Attitude:</u> Maintain a positive attitude, even on tough days. Positivity can improve your work performance and the work environment.

<u>Communication</u>: Good communication is key. Whether it's asking for help when you need it or keeping your team updated on your progress, clear and concise communication is crucial.

<u>Reliability:</u> Be someone your team can depend on. Meet your deadlines, show up on time, and follow through on your commitments.

<u>Continuous Learning:</u> Always be open to learning. Whether it's a new skill, a new piece of software, or a new way of looking at things, continuous learning can make you a more valuable employee.

Never Let a Bad Day Show at Work

We all have bad days, but it's important not to let them affect our work. If you're having a tough day, take a few moments to yourself, whether it's a quick walk outside or a few minutes of deep breathing. Remember, it's okay to ask for help if you're feeling overwhelmed.

Reflecting on Past Experiences

Looking back on my own experiences, there are things I did that were helpful and things I wish I had done differently. For example, I found that regularly updating my resume made it easier when it came time to apply for jobs. However, I wish I had spent more time networking and building relationships in my industry.

Remember, everyone's journey is different, and what works for one person might not work for another. The key is to keep learning, keep growing, and keep striving to be the best you can be. Good luck on your journey!

CHAPTER 7: THE INTERVIEW PROCESS

The Art of the Interview

An interview is more than just a formal conversation; it's an opportunity to showcase your skills, experiences, and personality to a potential employer. It's normal to feel nervous, but preparation is key. Here's how to make a lasting impression:

1. Research: Understand the company's mission, values, and culture. Familiarize yourself with the job description and align your skills and experiences with the requirements.

2. Practice: Anticipate common interview questions and practice your responses. Use the STAR method (Situation, Task, Action, Result) to structure your answers.
3. Dress Appropriately: Your attire should reflect the company's dress code. When in doubt, it's better to be overdressed than under dressed.
4. Arrive Early: Aim to arrive 10-15 minutes early. This shows respect for the interviewer's time and allows you to relax and gather your thoughts.
5. Body Language: Maintain eye contact, offer a firm handshake, and sit up straight. These non-verbal cues can convey confidence and professionalism.

The STAR Method

The STAR method is a structured way of responding to behavioral interview questions. Here's how I used it:

- Situation: I was working on a team project at my previous job where we were facing a tight deadline.
- Task: My task was to coordinate with team members and ensure the project was completed on time.
- Action: I created a detailed project plan, delegated tasks, and conducted daily check-ins to monitor progress.
- Result: We completed the project ahead of schedule and received positive feedback from our manager.

Using the STAR method helped me provide clear and concise answers, making me stand out from other applicants.

Navigating Nerves

Feeling nervous before an interview is completely normal. It's a sign that you care about the outcome. Here are some strategies to manage nerves:

- Preparation: The more prepared you are, the less nervous you'll feel. Research the company, review the job description, and practice your responses to common interview questions.
- Mindfulness: Practice deep breathing exercises or meditation before the interview to calm your mind.
- Perspective: Remember, an interview is just a conversation. It's an opportunity for you to learn more about the company and for the company to learn more about you.

Asking Questions

At the end of the interview, it's important to ask the interviewer a few questions. This shows your interest in the role and the company. Here are some examples:

- Can you describe the company culture?
- What does a typical day look like in this role?
- What opportunities for professional development does the company offer?
- How do you measure success in this role?

Remember, an interview is as much about you assessing the company as it is about the company assessing you. You want to ensure that the company is a good fit for you, just as much as you are a good fit for them.

Perseverance in the Face of Rejection

Rejection is a part of the job search process, and it's important to remember that a "no" is not always definitive. Here's how to navigate through it:

1. Don't Take It Personally: Remember, a rejection is not a reflection of your worth. There could be numerous reasons why you didn't get the job, many of which may have nothing to do with you.
2. Ask for Feedback: If possible, ask the interviewer for feedback. This can provide valuable insights into areas you might need to improve.
3. Reflect and Learn: Use the rejection as a learning opportunity. Reflect on your interview performance and identify areas where you could improve.
4. Stay Positive: Maintain a positive attitude. Job searching can be a long process, and it's important to stay motivated and optimistic.
5. Keep Applying: Don't let a rejection stop you from applying to other jobs. The right opportunity could be just around the corner.
6. Persistence Pays Off: A "no" now doesn't mean "no" forever. If you're still interested in the company, keep an eye on their job postings. A different role might open up that's a better fit for you.

Remember, every "no" brings you one step closer to a "yes". Keep trying, keep learning, and most importantly, keep believing in yourself. Your perseverance will pay off in the end.

In conclusion, a successful interview requires preparation, practice, and the right mindset. With these strategies, you'll be well on your way to making a positive impression and landing the job. Good luck!

CHAPTER 8: JOB HUNTING

Job hunting can be one of the most challenging and stressful experiences for young adults, especially when you're just starting out on your own or balancing college at the same time. Whether you're looking for a stepping stone job, part-time work for extra income, or a long-term career, the process requires patience, perseverance, and a strategic approach. This chapter will guide you through the essentials of job hunting, from finding good-paying jobs to avoiding scams, and provide practical tips to help you succeed.

Understanding Your Job Search Goals

Before diving into the job market, it's important to understand your goals. Are you looking for a temporary job to gain experience, a part-time job to support yourself while studying, or a full-time career in your field of interest? Clarifying your objectives will help you focus your search and tailor your applications accordingly.

Stepping Stone Jobs

Stepping stone jobs are positions that may not be your dream job but can provide valuable experience, skills, and networking opportunities. These jobs are often entry-level and can serve as a bridge to more advanced roles in the future.

Examples:

- Internships
- Administrative assistant roles
- Retail or customer service positions

Pros:

- Gain practical experience
- Build your resume
- Develop transferable skills

Cons:

- May not be highly paid
- Can be repetitive or mundane
- Limited long-term growth

Part-Time Jobs for Extra Income

Part-time jobs are ideal for students or those who need additional income without committing to full-time hours. These jobs offer flexibility and can help you manage your finances while pursuing other goals.

Examples:

- Barista or server
- Tutor or teaching assistant
- Freelance work (writing, graphic design, etc.)

Pros:

- Flexible hours
- Opportunity to earn extra income
- Can balance with studies or other commitments

Cons:

- Limited benefits
- May not offer career advancement
- Income can be inconsistent

Long-Term Careers

If you're ready to start building a long-term career, focus on finding positions that align with your skills, interests, and long-term goals. These jobs often require more experience and education but offer greater stability and growth potential.

Examples:

- Marketing coordinator
- Software developer
- Financial analyst

Pros:

- Career growth and advancement
- Higher earning potential
- Job stability and benefits

Cons:

- Competitive job market
- Requires relevant experience and education
- Longer application process

Searching for Good-Paying Jobs

Finding good-paying jobs requires a strategic approach and the use of various resources. Here are some effective methods to help you in your search:

Online Job Boards

Online job boards are a great starting point for job hunting. Websites like Indeed, LinkedIn, Glassdoor, and Monster offer a wide range of job listings across different industries and locations. You can filter your search based on your preferences, such as salary, job type, and location.

Tips:

- Set up job alerts to receive notifications for new listings
- Customize your resume and cover letter for each application
- Research companies before applying

Company Websites

Many companies post job openings directly on their websites. If you have specific companies in mind, regularly check their career pages for new opportunities. This approach shows your interest in the company and can give you an edge over other applicants.

Tips:

- Follow companies on social media to stay updated on job openings
- Network with current employees to learn about potential opportunities
- Tailor your application to align with the company's values and culture

Networking

Networking is one of the most effective ways to find job opportunities. Building relationships with professionals in your field can lead to job referrals and insider information about job openings. Attend industry events, join professional organizations, and connect with people on LinkedIn.

Tips:

- Attend networking events and job fairs
- Join industry-specific groups and forums
- Reach out to alumni from your college or university

Recruitment Agencies

Recruitment agencies can help match you with job opportunities that fit your skills and experience. These agencies work with employers to fill positions and can provide valuable insights into the job market.

Tips:

- Research reputable recruitment agencies in your industry
- Be clear about your job preferences and goals
- Follow up regularly with your recruiter

Avoiding Job Scams

Unfortunately, the job market is not without its pitfalls. Scammers often prey on job seekers, offering too-good-to-be-true opportunities that can lead to financial loss and identity theft. Here are some red flags to watch out for:

Too-Good-To-Be-True Listings

If a job listing promises high pay for minimal work or requires little to no experience, it may be a scam. Be cautious of listings that guarantee quick wealth or extravagant benefits.

Red Flags:

- High salary for entry-level positions

- Vague job descriptions
- No required qualifications or experience

Lack of Official Interview Process

Legitimate employers typically conduct interviews and require candidates to fill out proper paperwork. If someone offers you a job without an official interview or asks for personal information upfront, it's likely a scam.

Red Flags:

- No interview or formal hiring process
- Requests for personal information (e.g., Social Security number) early on
- Offers to send money for purchases or training

Upfront Fees

Be wary of job listings that require you to pay upfront fees for training, equipment, or background checks. Legitimate employers do not ask candidates to pay for these expenses.

Red Flags:

- Requests for payment to secure the job
- Promises of reimbursement after payment
- Pressure to act quickly

Unprofessional Communication

Scammers often use unprofessional communication methods, such as poorly written emails, generic greetings, and lack of contact information. Legitimate employers typically use official company email addresses and provide clear contact details.

Red Flags:

- Emails from free email services (e.g., Gmail, Yahoo)
- Poor grammar and spelling
- Lack of company contact information

Tips for a Successful Job Hunt

Job hunting can be challenging, but with the right approach, you can increase your chances of success. Here are some tips to help you navigate the job market:

Tailor Your Resume and Cover Letter

Customize your resume and cover letter for each job application. Highlight your relevant skills and experience, and explain why you're a good fit for the position. Use keywords from the job description to make your application stand out.

Example: If you're applying for a marketing coordinator position, emphasize your experience with social media management, content creation, and data analysis.

Prepare for Interviews

Interviews are a crucial part of the job search process. Prepare by researching the company, practicing common interview questions, and dressing professionally. Be ready to discuss your skills, experience, and why you're interested in the position.

Example: Practice answering questions like "Tell me about yourself," "Why do you want to work here?" and "What are your strengths and weaknesses?"

Be Persistent

Job hunting can be a long and challenging process, but don't give up. Stay persistent, keep applying, and continue improving your skills and resume. Rejection is a normal part of the process, and each application brings you closer to finding the right job.

Example: If you receive a rejection, ask for feedback to understand how you can improve for future applications.

Exploring Different Job Opportunities

Don't limit yourself to traditional job roles. Explore different opportunities to find what suits you best. You might discover a passion for something you hadn't considered before.

Freelancing

Freelancing offers flexibility and the opportunity to work on a variety of projects. If you have skills in writing, graphic design, programming, or other areas, freelancing can be a great way to earn income and build your portfolio.

Pros:

- Flexible schedule
- Opportunity to work on diverse projects
- Potential for high earnings

Cons:

- Inconsistent income
- Requires self-discipline and time management
- No employee benefits

Gig Economy Jobs

The gig economy offers short-term, flexible jobs that can provide extra income. Platforms like Uber, Lyft, TaskRabbit, and Fiverr connect workers with clients looking for specific services.

Pros:

- Flexible hours
- Variety of job opportunities
- Quick way to earn money

Cons:

- Inconsistent income
- Lack of job security
- No employee benefits

Internships and Apprenticeships

Internships and apprenticeships provide hands-on experience and can lead to full-time job offers. These positions are often available in various industries and can help you build valuable skills and connections.

Pros:

- Gain practical experience

- Build your professional network
- Potential for full-time job offers

Cons:

- Often low-paying or unpaid
- Temporary positions
- May require a significant time commitment

Balancing Job Hunting with College

If you're in college, balancing job hunting with your studies can be challenging. Here are some tips to help you manage both:

Time Management

Effective time management is crucial for balancing job hunting with college. Create a schedule that allocates time for studying, job applications, and interviews. Prioritize your tasks and set realistic goals for each day.

Tips:

- Use a planner or digital calendar to organize your schedule.
- Break tasks into smaller, manageable steps.
- Set aside specific times for job hunting activities.

Leveraging Campus Resources

Many colleges offer resources to help students with job hunting. Take advantage of career services, job fairs, and networking events. These resources can provide valuable guidance and connect you with potential employers.

Tips:

- Visit your college's career center for resume reviews and mock interviews.
- Attend job fairs and networking events to meet employers.
- Join student organizations related to your field of interest.

Online Learning and Certifications

Enhancing your skills through online courses and certifications can make you a more competitive job candidate. Platforms like Coursera, Udemy, and LinkedIn Learning offer courses in various subjects that can complement your college education.

Tips:

- Identify skills that are in demand in your desired field.
- Enroll in relevant online courses and complete certifications.
- Add these new skills and certifications to your resume.

Recognizing and Avoiding Job Scams

The job market can be a minefield of scams and fraudulent job listings. It's important to recognize the signs of a scam and protect yourself from falling victim.

Common Job Scams

1. Fake Job Listings: Scammers create fake job postings to collect personal information or money from unsuspecting job seekers.
2. Phishing Scams: Scammers send emails that appear to be from legitimate companies, asking for personal information or directing you to fake websites. (Do not click on random links, it will open yourself up for a virus or someone getting ahold of personal information. Type the web address into the browser directly to check it out.)
3. Work-From-Home Scams: Scammers promise high-paying work-from-home jobs but require upfront fees for training or equipment.

How to Spot a Scam

1. Too-Good-To-Be-True Offers: If a job offer seems too good to be true, it probably is. Be wary of high salaries for minimal work or jobs that require no experience.
2. Lack of Contact Information: Legitimate job listings should include clear contact information for the employer. Be cautious of listings with vague or missing details.

3. Requests for Personal Information: Never provide personal information, such as your Social Security number or bank account details, early in the application process.
4. Upfront Fees: Legitimate employers do not ask for money upfront. Be wary of job listings that require payment for training, equipment, or background checks.

Protecting Yourself

1. Research the Company: Before applying, research the company to ensure it is legitimate. Check their website, read reviews, and look for any red flags.
2. Verify Job Listings: If you receive a job offer, verify it by contacting the company directly. Use contact information from the company's official website.
3. Trust Your Instincts: If something feels off about a job listing or offer, trust your instincts and proceed with caution.

Building a Strong Job Application

A strong job application can set you apart from other candidates. Here are some tips to help you create a compelling resume and cover letter:

Crafting a Compelling Resume

Your resume is your first impression on potential employers. Make sure it highlights your skills, experience, and accomplishments in a clear and concise manner.

Tips:

- Use a clean, professional layout.
- Include relevant work experience, education, and skills.
- Use action verbs to describe your accomplishments.
- Quantify your achievements with numbers and metrics.

Example: Instead of saying "Managed social media accounts," say "Increased social media engagement by 30% through targeted content strategies."

Writing an Effective Cover Letter

A cover letter allows you to explain why you're a good fit for the position and showcase your personality. Tailor each cover letter to the specific job and company.

Tips:

- Address the hiring manager by name if possible.
- Start with a strong opening that grabs attention.
- Highlight your relevant skills and experience.
- Explain why you're interested in the position and the company.
- End with a call to action, such as requesting an interview.

Example: "Dear [Hiring Manager's Name],

I am excited to apply for the marketing coordinator position at [Company Name]. With a background in social media management and content creation, I am confident in my ability to contribute to your team's success. I am particularly drawn to [Company Name] because of your innovative approach to digital marketing and commitment to community engagement.

I look forward to the opportunity to discuss how my skills and experience align with your needs. Thank you for considering my application.

Sincerely, [Your Name]"

Preparing for Job Interviews

Interviews are a crucial part of the job search process. Preparing thoroughly can help you make a positive impression and increase your chances of getting hired.

Researching the Company

Before your interview, research the company to understand its mission, values, and culture. This will help you tailor your responses and show that you're genuinely interested in the position.

Tips:

- Visit the company's website and read about their history, mission, and values.
- Follow the company on social media to stay updated on their latest news and initiatives.
- Read reviews from current and former employees on sites like Glassdoor.

Practicing Common Interview Questions

Practice answering common interview questions to build your confidence and improve your responses. Consider using the STAR method (Situation, Task, Action, Result) to structure your answers.

Common Questions:

- "Tell me about yourself."
- "Why do you want to work here?"
- "What are your strengths and weaknesses?"
- "Describe a challenging situation and how you handled it."

Example: "One challenging situation I faced was when our team was behind on a project deadline. I took the initiative to organize a meeting, delegate tasks, and set clear priorities. As a result, we were able to complete the project on time and received positive feedback from the client."

Dressing Professionally

First impressions matter, and dressing professionally can help you make a positive impact. Choose attire that is appropriate for the company's culture and the position you're applying for.

Tips:

- Research the company's dress code and dress one step above it.
- Choose clean, well-fitting clothes that make you feel confident.
- Pay attention to grooming and personal hygiene.

Following Up After the Interview

After your interview, send a thank-you email to express your appreciation and reiterate your interest in the position. This shows professionalism and keeps you top of mind with the hiring manager.

Example: "Dear [Interviewer's Name],

Thank you for the opportunity to interview for the marketing coordinator position at [Company Name]. I enjoyed learning more about your team and the exciting projects you're working on. I am enthusiastic about the possibility of contributing to your company's success.

Thank you again for your time and consideration.

Sincerely, [Your Name]"

Staying Motivated During the Job Hunt

Job hunting can be a long and challenging process, but staying motivated is key to success. Here are some strategies to keep your spirits high:

Set Realistic Goals

Set achievable goals for your job search, such as applying to a certain number of jobs each week or attending networking events. Celebrate small victories along the way to stay motivated.

Tips:

- Break down your job search into manageable tasks.
- Track your progress and celebrate milestones.
- Stay positive and focus on what you can control.

Take Care of Yourself

Job hunting can be stressful, so it's important to take care of your physical and mental well-being. Make time for activities that help you relax and recharge.

Tips:

- Exercise regularly to reduce stress and boost your mood.
- Practice mindfulness or meditation to stay focused and calm.
- Spend time with friends and family for support and encouragement.

Seek Support

Don't hesitate to seek support from friends, family, or mentors. They can provide valuable advice, encouragement, and a fresh perspective on your job search.

Tips:

- Join a job search support group or online community.
- Reach out to mentors for guidance and feedback.
- Share your progress and challenges with trusted friends and family.

Final Thoughts

Job hunting can be a daunting and often overwhelming process, especially for young adults stepping into the workforce for the first time. The journey is filled with challenges, from crafting the perfect resume to navigating interviews and avoiding scams. However, it's important to stay persistent and maintain a positive outlook. Each application, interview, and even rejection is a learning experience that brings you closer to your goal. Use good judgment, be open to trying different roles, and remember that finding the right job takes time. With patience, resilience, and a proactive approach, you can successfully navigate the job market and find a position that aligns with your skills and aspirations.

CHAPTER 9: JUGGLING ACT

Introduction

In today's fast-paced world, many young adults find themselves working multiple jobs to make ends meet, gain experience, or achieve their financial goals. While juggling multiple jobs can be challenging, it is also an opportunity to develop valuable skills, build a strong work ethic, and demonstrate your worth. This chapter will provide practical tips for managing multiple jobs, excelling in each role, maintaining a positive attitude, and working towards career advancement. We'll also explore strategies for continuous improvement and personal growth, ensuring you stay motivated and independent.

Section 1: Effective Time Management

One of the most critical aspects of juggling multiple jobs is managing your time effectively. Here are some strategies to help you stay organized and make the most of your time:

1. Create a Schedule: Use a planner or digital calendar to create a detailed schedule that includes your work hours, commute times, and personal commitments. Block out specific times for each job and ensure there is no overlap.
2. Prioritize Tasks: Identify the most important tasks for each job and prioritize them. Focus on completing high-priority tasks first to ensure you meet deadlines and expectations.
3. Set Realistic Goals: Set achievable goals for each job and break them down into smaller, manageable tasks. This will help you stay focused and motivated.
4. Use Time Wisely: Make the most of your downtime by using it for productive activities, such as planning your day, reviewing tasks, or learning new skills. Avoid wasting time on unproductive activities.
5. Avoid Multitasking: While it may seem efficient, multitasking can reduce your productivity and increase stress. Focus on one task at a time to ensure you complete it to the best of your ability.

Section 2: Maintaining High Performance

To excel in each of your jobs, it's essential to maintain high performance and demonstrate your commitment. Here are some tips to help you do your best at each job:

1. Understand Expectations: Clearly understand the expectations and responsibilities of each job. Communicate with your supervisors to ensure you know what is required of you.
2. Stay Organized: Keep your workspace organized and free of clutter. This will help you stay focused and efficient.
3. Be Proactive: Take the initiative to identify and address potential issues before they become problems. Offer solutions and suggestions to improve processes and outcomes.
4. Seek Feedback: Regularly seek feedback from your supervisors and colleagues. Use their input to improve your performance and address any areas of concern.
5. Stay Positive: Maintain a positive attitude, even during challenging times. A positive mindset can boost your productivity and help you overcome obstacles.

Section 3: Managing Stress and Avoiding Burnout

Working multiple jobs can be stressful, and it's essential to manage stress effectively to avoid burnout. Here are some strategies to help you stay balanced and healthy:

1. Practice Self-Care: Make time for self-care activities, such as exercise, meditation, and hobbies. Taking care of your physical and mental well-being is crucial for maintaining energy and focus.
2. Set Boundaries: Establish clear boundaries between work and personal time. Avoid bringing work-related stress into your personal life and vice versa.
3. Take Breaks: Schedule regular breaks throughout your day to rest and recharge. Short breaks can improve your productivity and reduce stress.
4. Stay Connected: Maintain a support network of friends, family, and colleagues. Talking to others about your experiences can provide emotional support and valuable insights.
5. Seek Professional Help: If you feel overwhelmed or stressed, consider seeking help from a mental health professional. They can provide strategies and support to help you manage stress effectively.

Section 4: Never Let a Bad Day Show at Work

Everyone has bad days, but it's important not to let them affect your performance or interactions at work. Here are some tips for maintaining professionalism and a positive attitude, even on tough days:

1. Leave Personal Issues at the Door: When you arrive at work, make a conscious effort to leave personal issues behind. Focus on your tasks and responsibilities.

2. Practice Mindfulness: Use mindfulness techniques, such as deep breathing or meditation, to stay calm and centered. This can help you manage stress and maintain a positive attitude.
3. Find a Positive Outlet: If you're having a bad day, find a positive outlet to release your emotions. This could be talking to a trusted colleague, taking a short walk, or listening to music.
4. Stay Professional: Regardless of how you feel, always maintain a professional demeanor. Treat your colleagues and customers with respect and courtesy.
5. Focus on Solutions: Instead of dwelling on problems, focus on finding solutions. This proactive approach can help you overcome challenges and improve your mood.

Section 5: Working Hard to Achieve Goals and Get Promoted

Hard work and dedication are key to achieving your career goals and earning promotions. Here are some strategies to help you stand out and advance in your career:

1. Set Clear Goals: Define your career goals and create a plan to achieve them. Break down your goals into actionable steps and track your progress.
2. Show Initiative: Take on additional responsibilities and volunteer for challenging projects. Demonstrating your willingness to go above and beyond can set you apart from your peers.

3. Develop Skills: Continuously seek opportunities to develop new skills and improve existing ones. Attend workshops, take online courses, and seek mentorship to enhance your knowledge and abilities.
4. Network: Build relationships with colleagues, supervisors, and industry professionals. Networking can open doors to new opportunities and provide valuable insights and support.
5. Demonstrate Reliability: Be dependable and consistent in your work. Show up on time, meet deadlines, and deliver high-quality results.
6. Communicate Effectively: Develop strong communication skills to convey your ideas clearly and build positive relationships with colleagues and supervisors.
7. Seek Feedback and Act on It: Regularly seek feedback on your performance and use it to make improvements. Show that you are open to constructive criticism and committed to growth.

Section 6: Continuous Improvement and Learning

To succeed in multiple jobs and advance in your career, it's essential to embrace continuous improvement and lifelong learning. Here are some tips to help you stay on the path of growth:

1. Stay Curious: Cultivate a curious mindset and seek to learn new things. Ask questions, explore new topics, and stay informed about industry trends.

2. Set Personal Development Goals: Identify areas where you want to improve and set specific goals for personal development. Create a plan to achieve these goals and track your progress.
3. Learn from Mistakes: View mistakes as opportunities for learning and growth. Reflect on what went wrong, identify lessons learned, and apply them to future situations.
4. Seek Mentorship: Find mentors who can provide guidance, support, and valuable insights. Learn from their experiences and seek their advice on your career development.
5. Stay Adaptable: Be open to change and willing to adapt to new situations. Flexibility and adaptability are essential skills in today's dynamic work environment.

Section 7: Additional Tips and Tricks for Young Adults

Here are some additional tips and tricks to help young adults succeed in juggling multiple jobs and achieving independence:

1. Stay Organized: Use tools such as planners, to-do lists, and digital apps to stay organized and manage your tasks effectively.
2. Manage Finances Wisely: Create a budget and track your expenses to ensure you are managing your fi-

nances responsibly. Save a portion of your income for future goals and emergencies.
3. Maintain a Healthy Work-Life Balance: Strive to balance your work commitments with personal time. Make time for activities that bring you joy and relaxation.
4. Stay Motivated: Keep your long-term goals in mind and stay motivated by celebrating small achievements along the way.
5. Build a Support Network: Surround yourself with supportive friends, family, and colleagues who can provide encouragement and assistance when needed.
6. Practice Effective Communication: Develop strong communication skills to build positive relationships and resolve conflicts effectively.
7. Stay Resilient: Embrace challenges and setbacks as opportunities for growth. Stay resilient and maintain a positive attitude, even in difficult times.

Conclusion

Juggling multiple jobs as a young adult can be demanding, but with the right strategies and mindset, it is possible to succeed and thrive. By managing your time effectively, maintaining high performance, managing stress, and continuously improving, you can achieve your career goals and demonstrate your worth. Remember to stay organized, motivated, and resilient, and seek support when needed. With dedication and hard work, you can navigate the challenges of multiple jobs and build a strong foundation for your future independence and success.

CHAPTER 10: BUDGETING BLUEPRINT

Introduction

Budgeting is a fundamental skill that can significantly impact your financial well-being and independence. For young adults, especially those with limited income and time, and those attending college, mastering the art of budgeting is crucial. This chapter will delve into the importance of budgeting, provide tips on creating and sticking to a budget, and offer strategies for saving for specific goals, such as a vacation. By the end of this chapter, you'll have a comprehensive understanding of how to manage your finances effectively and achieve your financial goals.

Section 1: The Importance of Budgeting

Budgeting is the process of creating a plan to manage your income and expenses. It helps you allocate your resources efficiently, avoid overspending, and save for future goals. Here are some key reasons why budgeting is essential:

1. Financial Control: Budgeting gives you control over your finances. It allows you to track your income and expenses, ensuring you live within your means.
2. Goal Achievement: A budget helps you set and achieve financial goals, such as saving for a vacation, paying off debt, or building an emergency fund.
3. Debt Management: By budgeting, you can allocate funds to pay off debt systematically, reducing financial stress and interest payments.
4. Emergency Preparedness: A budget helps you build an emergency fund, providing a financial cushion for unexpected expenses.
5. Spending Awareness: Budgeting increases your awareness of spending habits, helping you identify areas where you can cut back and save money.
6. Financial Independence: Effective budgeting is a step towards financial independence, allowing you to make informed financial decisions and avoid reliance on others.

Section 2: Tips on Creating a Budget

Creating a budget involves several steps, from assessing your financial situation to tracking your expenses. Here are some tips to help you create an effective budget:

1. Assess Your Income: Start by calculating your total monthly income. Include all sources of income, such as wages, scholarships, financial aid, and any side gigs.
2. List Your Expenses: Make a comprehensive list of all your monthly expenses. Categorize them into fixed expenses (e.g., rent, utilities) and variable expenses (e.g., groceries, entertainment).
3. Set Financial Goals: Define your short-term and long-term financial goals. Short-term goals might include saving for a vacation, while long-term goals could involve paying off student loans or building an emergency fund.
4. Allocate Funds: Allocate your income to cover your expenses and financial goals. Use the 50/30/20 rule as a guideline: 50% of your income for necessities, 30% for discretionary spending, and 20% for savings and debt repayment.
5. Track Your Spending: Use budgeting apps or spreadsheets to track your spending. Regularly review your expenses to ensure you stay within your budget.
6. Adjust as Needed: Be flexible and adjust your budget as needed. Life circumstances can change, and your budget should reflect those changes.

Section 3: Strategies for Sticking to a Budget

Creating a budget is only the first step; sticking to it is where the real challenge lies. Here are some strategies to help you stay on track:

1. Automate Savings: Set up automatic transfers from your checking account to your savings account. This ensures you save consistently without having to think about it.
2. Use Cash for Discretionary Spending: Withdraw a set amount of cash for discretionary spending each week. Once the cash is gone, avoid using credit or debit cards for non-essential purchases.
3. Review Your Budget Regularly: Schedule regular budget reviews to assess your progress and make adjustments. This helps you stay accountable and identify any areas where you may be overspending.
4. Avoid Impulse Purchases: Before making a purchase, ask yourself if it's a need or a want. Delay non-essential purchases to avoid impulse buying.
5. Find Affordable Alternatives: Look for affordable alternatives for entertainment, dining, and shopping. For example, use student discounts, attend free events, and shop during sales.
6. Stay Motivated: Keep your financial goals in mind and celebrate small achievements. Staying motivated will help you stick to your budget and make progress towards your goals.

Section 4: Budgeting for Specific Goals: Saving for a Vacation

Saving for a vacation requires careful planning and budgeting. Here are some steps to help you save for your dream trip:

1. Set a Vacation Goal: Determine your vacation destination, duration, and estimated costs. Include expenses such as transportation, accommodation, food, activities, and souvenirs.
2. Create a Vacation Fund: Open a separate savings account dedicated to your vacation fund. This helps you keep your vacation savings separate from your regular savings.
3. Set a Savings Target: Calculate how much you need to save each month to reach your vacation goal. Divide the total estimated cost by the number of months until your trip.
4. Cut Back on Non-Essential Expenses: Identify areas where you can cut back on non-essential expenses and redirect those funds to your vacation savings. For example, reduce dining out, entertainment, and shopping expenses.
5. Find Additional Income Sources: Look for ways to earn extra income, such as taking on a part-time job, freelancing, or selling items you no longer need. Use this additional income to boost your vacation fund.
6. Track Your Progress: Regularly track your savings progress and adjust your budget as needed. Stay mo-

tivated by visualizing your vacation and the experiences you'll enjoy.

Section 5: Budgeting for Young Adults with Limited Income and Time

For young adults with limited income and time, budgeting can be particularly challenging. Here are some strategies to help you manage your finances effectively:

1. Prioritize Essential Expenses: Focus on covering your essential expenses first, such as rent, utilities, groceries, and transportation. Ensure these expenses are accounted for in your budget.
2. Utilize Financial Aid and Scholarships: If you're attending college, take advantage of financial aid, scholarships, and grants. These can help reduce your educational expenses and free up funds for other needs.
3. Live Within Your Means: Avoid lifestyle inflation and live within your means. Resist the temptation to spend money on non-essential items or activities that you can't afford.
4. Take Advantage of Student Discounts: Many businesses offer discounts to students. Always carry your student ID and ask about discounts when shopping, dining, or using services.
5. Share Expenses: Consider sharing expenses with roommates or friends. This can help reduce your housing, utility, and grocery costs.

6. Plan Meals and Cook at Home: Plan your meals in advance and cook at home to save money on food. Avoid eating out frequently, as it can quickly add up.
7. Use Public Transportation: If you live in an area with reliable public transportation, use it instead of owning a car. This can save you money on gas, insurance, and maintenance.
8. Seek Part-Time Work: Look for part-time jobs or freelance opportunities that fit your schedule. Even a few extra hours of work each week can provide additional income to cover expenses and save.

Section 6: Practical Examples and Personal Advice

To provide practical insights, let's explore some examples and personal advice on budgeting for young adults:

Example 1: Meal Planning and Grocery Shopping:

- Strategy: Plan your meals for the week and create a shopping list based on your meal plan. Stick to the list to avoid impulse purchases.
- Personal Advice: I found that meal planning not only saved me money but also reduced food waste. I would cook in bulk and freeze portions for later, which made it easier to stick to my budget.

Example 2: Utilizing Campus Resources:

- Strategy: Take advantage of free campus resources, such as the library, gym, and student events. These

resources can help you save money on books, fitness memberships, and entertainment.
- Personal Advice: During my college years, I regularly used the campus gym and attended free workshops and events. This allowed me to stay active and engaged without spending extra money.

Example 3: Finding Affordable Housing:

- Strategy: Look for affordable housing options, such as shared apartments or dormitories. Consider living with roommates to split rent and utility costs.
- Personal Advice: I chose to live with roommates throughout college, which significantly reduced my housing expenses. We also shared household chores and groceries, making it a cost-effective arrangement.

Example 4: Part-Time Work and Freelancing:

- Strategy: Seek part-time jobs or freelance opportunities that align with your skills and schedule. Use the extra income to cover expenses and save.
- Personal Advice: I worked part-time as a tutor and freelance writer during college. This not only provided additional income but also helped me develop valuable skills and build my resume.

Example 5: Budgeting and Tracking Expenses:

- Strategy: Create a detailed budget and track your expenses regularly. Use budgeting apps or spreadsheets to monitor your spending and identify areas for improvement.
- Personal Advice: Keeping a budget was crucial for me to stay on track with my financial goals. I reviewed my expenses weekly and adjusted my spending habits as needed to ensure I was saving enough.

Section 7: Overcoming Financial Challenges

While saving money as a young adult can be challenging, it's important to stay motivated and resilient. Here are some tips for overcoming common financial challenges:

1. Stay Positive and Focused: Financial setbacks are inevitable, but maintaining a positive attitude and staying focused on your goals can help you overcome them.
2. Seek Support and Advice: Don't hesitate to seek support from family, friends, or financial advisors. They can provide valuable insights and encouragement.
3. Be Flexible and Adaptable: Be willing to adjust your budget and strategies as needed. Life circumstances can change, and being adaptable will help you navigate financial challenges more effectively.
4. Celebrate Small Wins: Recognize and celebrate your financial achievements, no matter how small. This will keep you motivated and reinforce positive financial habits.

Conclusion:

Budgeting is a powerful tool that can help you take control of your finances, achieve your goals, and build a secure future. For young adults, especially those with limited income and time, mastering budgeting basics is essential. By understanding the importance of budgeting, creating a realistic budget, and implementing strategies to stick to it, you can navigate financial challenges and make informed decisions.

Remember, budgeting is not about restricting yourself but about making conscious choices that align with your financial goals. Whether you're saving for a vacation, paying off debt, or building an emergency fund, a well-planned budget can guide you towards financial independence and stability. Stay disciplined, stay motivated, and continuously educate yourself about personal finance. With dedication and effort, you can achieve your financial aspirations and enjoy the peace of mind that comes with financial security.

CHAPTER 11: CREDIT CREATION

Credit is a fundamental aspect of modern financial life, influencing everything from your ability to rent an apartment to securing a mortgage for your first home. Understanding how credit works, why it is important, and how to manage it responsibly is crucial for achieving financial independence and stability. This chapter will delve into the intricacies of credit, provide practical advice on building and maintaining good credit, and share personal experiences to illustrate the impact of credit on your financial journey.

What is Credit?

Credit is essentially the ability to borrow money or access goods and services with the understanding that you will pay for them later. It is based on the trust that you will repay the borrowed amount, often with interest, within a specified period. Credit can come in various forms, including credit cards, personal loans, mortgages, and lines of credit.

Types of Credit

1. Revolving Credit: This type of credit allows you to borrow up to a certain limit and repay it over time. Credit cards are a common example of revolving credit. You can use the credit repeatedly as long as you stay within the credit limit and make timely payments.
2. Installment Credit: With installment credit, you borrow a fixed amount of money and repay it in equal installments over a set period. Examples include auto loans, student loans, and mortgages.
3. Open Credit: This type of credit requires you to pay the full balance each month. Utility bills and charge cards are examples of open credit.

How Credit Works

Credit works on the principle of borrowing and repaying. When you use credit, you are essentially borrowing money from a lender with the promise to repay it later. The terms of repayment, including the interest rate and repayment schedule, are outlined in the credit agreement.

Key Components of Credit

1. Credit Limit: The maximum amount you can borrow on a credit account. For credit cards, this is the maximum balance you can carry.
2. Interest Rate: The cost of borrowing money, expressed as a percentage of the amount borrowed. Interest rates can be fixed or variable.
3. Minimum Payment: The smallest amount you must pay each month to keep your account in good standing. Paying only the minimum can result in high interest charges over time.
4. Credit Report: A detailed record of your credit history, including your borrowing and repayment activities. Credit reports are maintained by credit bureaus.
5. Credit Score: A numerical representation of your creditworthiness, based on information in your credit report. Credit scores range from 300 to 850, with higher scores indicating better credit.

Why Credit is Important

Credit plays a vital role in your financial life. It affects your ability to borrow money, rent an apartment, get a job, and even secure insurance. Here are some reasons why credit is important:

1. Access to Loans and Credit: Good credit makes it easier to qualify for loans and credit cards with favorable terms, such as lower interest rates and higher credit limits.
2. Lower Interest Rates: Lenders view individuals with good credit as less risky, which can result in lower interest rates on loans and credit cards. This can save you money over time.
3. Housing Opportunities: Landlords often check credit reports to assess the reliability of potential tenants. Good credit can increase your chances of securing a rental property.
4. Employment Opportunities: Some employers check credit reports as part of the hiring process, especially for positions that involve financial responsibilities.
5. Insurance Premiums: Insurance companies may use credit information to determine premiums. Good credit can lead to lower insurance costs.

The Consequences of Abusing Credit

While credit can be a powerful financial tool, it can also lead to significant problems if mismanaged. Abusing credit can result in debt, financial stress, and long-term damage to your credit score. Here are some potential consequences of abusing credit:

1. High-Interest Debt: Carrying high balances on credit cards can lead to substantial interest charges, making it difficult to pay off the debt.

2. Credit Score Damage: Late payments, maxed-out credit cards, and defaulting on loans can significantly lower your credit score, making it harder to qualify for credit in the future.
3. Financial Stress: Managing high levels of debt can cause financial stress and impact your overall well-being.
4. Limited Financial Opportunities: Poor credit can limit your ability to access loans, rent housing, and secure employment.
5. Legal Consequences: In extreme cases, unpaid debts can lead to legal actions, such as wage garnishments or liens on your property.

Avoiding Frequent Credit Applications

Applying for credit too often can negatively impact your credit score. Each time you apply for credit, a hard inquiry is recorded on your credit report. Multiple hard inquiries within a short period can lower your credit score and signal to lenders that you may be a high-risk borrower.

Tips to Avoid Frequent Credit Applications

1. Research Before Applying: Before applying for credit, research the requirements and ensure you meet the criteria. This can help you avoid unnecessary applications.
2. Space Out Applications: If you need to apply for multiple credit accounts, try to space out the applications

over several months to minimize the impact on your credit score.
3. Use Prequalification Tools: Some lenders offer prequalification tools that allow you to check your eligibility without affecting your credit score.

How Creditors Use Credit for Lending

Creditors use your credit report and credit score to assess your creditworthiness and determine whether to approve your credit application. They consider several factors, including your payment history, credit utilization, length of credit history, types of credit, and recent credit inquiries.

Key Factors Creditors Consider

1. Payment History: Your track record of making on-time payments is one of the most important factors in determining your creditworthiness.
2. Credit Utilization: This is the ratio of your current credit card balances to your credit limits. Lower credit utilization indicates responsible credit management.
3. Length of Credit History: A longer credit history provides more information about your borrowing and repayment behavior.
4. Types of Credit: Having a mix of credit accounts, such as credit cards, installment loans, and mortgages, can positively impact your credit score.
5. Recent Credit Inquiries: Multiple recent credit inquiries can indicate a higher risk to lenders.

The Impact of Credit on Your Life

Credit affects various aspects of your life, from your financial opportunities to your overall well-being. Here are some ways credit can impact you:

1. Financial Opportunities: Good credit opens doors to better financial opportunities, such as lower interest rates, higher credit limits, and access to premium credit cards.
2. Housing: Your credit history can influence your ability to rent an apartment or qualify for a mortgage. Landlords and lenders use credit information to assess your reliability.
3. Employment: Some employers check credit reports as part of the hiring process. A good credit history can enhance your job prospects.
4. Insurance: Insurance companies may use credit information to determine premiums. Good credit can lead to lower insurance costs.
5. Peace of Mind: Managing credit responsibly can reduce financial stress and provide peace of mind, knowing you have access to credit when needed.

Building Credit from Scratch

Building credit from scratch can be challenging, but it's essential for establishing a strong financial foundation. Here are some steps to help you start building credit:

1. Open a Secured Credit Card: A secured credit card requires a cash deposit as collateral, which serves as your credit limit. Using a secured card responsibly can help you build credit.
2. Become an Authorized User: Ask a family member or friend with good credit to add you as an authorized user on their credit card. This can help you build credit without the responsibility of managing the account.
3. Apply for a Credit-Builder Loan: Some financial institutions offer credit-builder loans designed to help individuals build credit. The loan amount is held in a savings account, and you make monthly payments until the loan is paid off.
4. Pay Bills on Time: Consistently paying your bills on time is crucial for building a positive credit history.
5. Monitor Your Credit: Regularly check your credit report to ensure the information is accurate and to track your progress.

Personal Experiences with Credit

Sharing personal experiences can provide valuable insights into the impact of credit on your financial journey. Here are some examples of things that hurt my credit and things that helped it:

Things That Hurt My Credit

1. Late Payments: Early in my financial journey, I missed a few credit card payments due to poor bud-

geting and lack of organization. These late payments significantly lowered my credit score and stayed on my credit report for several years. It was a hard lesson in the importance of paying bills on time.
2. High Credit Utilization: At one point, I maxed out my credit cards, which led to a high credit utilization ratio. This negatively impacted my credit score and made it difficult to get approved for new credit. It took time and disciplined repayment to bring my balances down and improve my credit utilization.
3. Applying for Multiple Credit Cards: In an attempt to build credit quickly, I applied for several credit cards within a short period. This resulted in multiple hard inquiries on my credit report, which temporarily lowered my credit score. I learned that spacing out credit applications is crucial to maintaining a healthy credit score.

Things That Helped My Credit

1. Consistent On-Time Payments: After experiencing the consequences of late payments, I made it a priority to pay all my bills on time. Setting up automatic payments and reminders helped ensure I never missed a due date. Over time, this consistent behavior positively impacted my credit score.
2. Paying Down Debt: I focused on paying down my credit card balances to reduce my credit utilization ratio. By making more than the minimum payments

and prioritizing high-interest debt, I was able to lower my balances and improve my credit score.
3. Diversifying Credit Accounts: I diversified my credit portfolio by taking out a small personal loan and responsibly managing a mix of credit accounts. This demonstrated to lenders that I could handle different types of credit, which positively influenced my credit score.
4. Monitoring My Credit: Regularly checking my credit report allowed me to catch errors and track my progress. I used free credit monitoring services to stay informed about changes to my credit report and score.

How Credit Scores Work

Credit scores are numerical representations of your creditworthiness, based on information in your credit report. They range from 300 to 850, with higher scores indicating better credit. Credit scores are calculated using various factors, each contributing a different percentage to the overall score.

Factors Affecting Credit Scores

1. Payment History (35%): Your history of on-time payments is the most significant factor in determining your credit score. Late payments can have a substantial negative impact.
2. Credit Utilization (30%): This is the ratio of your current credit card balances to your credit limits. Keep-

ing your credit utilization below 30% is recommended.

3. Length of Credit History (15%): The longer your credit history, the better. This factor considers the age of your oldest account, the age of your newest account, and the average age of all your accounts.
4. Types of Credit (10%): Having a mix of credit accounts, such as credit cards, installment loans, and mortgages, can positively impact your credit score.
5. New Credit (10%): Opening multiple new credit accounts in a short period can lower your credit score. Space out applications to minimize the impact.

Credit Freezes

A credit freeze, also known as a security freeze, is a tool that allows you to restrict access to your credit report. This can help protect you from identity theft and fraud, as it prevents new creditors from accessing your credit report without your permission.

How to Place a Credit Freeze

1. Contact Credit Bureaus: To place a credit freeze, you need to contact each of the three major credit bureaus (Equifax, Experian, and TransUnion) individually. You can do this online, by phone, or by mail.
2. Provide Information: You will need to provide personal information, such as your name, address, date of birth, and Social Security number, to verify your identity.

3. Receive a PIN: Each credit bureau will provide you with a unique PIN or password that you will use to lift or temporarily remove the freeze.

Pros and Cons of Credit Freezes
Pros:

- Protection from Identity Theft: A credit freeze can prevent new accounts from being opened in your name without your permission.
- Free to Place and Lift: Credit freezes are free to place and lift, making them an accessible tool for protecting your credit.

Cons:

- Inconvenience: If you need to apply for credit, you will need to temporarily lift the freeze, which can be inconvenient.
- Does Not Affect Existing Accounts: A credit freeze does not affect your existing credit accounts, so you still need to monitor them for fraudulent activity.

Conclusion

Understanding credit and managing it responsibly is crucial for building a strong financial foundation. By learning how credit works, recognizing its importance, and avoiding common pitfalls, you can achieve financial stability and open doors to better opportunities. Remember, building and maintaining good credit takes time and effort, but the benefits are well worth it. Stay informed, make smart financial decisions, and use credit as a tool to achieve your financial goals.

CHAPTER 12: INVESTMENT INSIGHTS

Introduction
Welcome to the exciting world of investing! Whether you're a college student, a recent graduate, or someone just starting their career, understanding how to invest can significantly impact your financial well-being. In this chapter, we'll break down the basics of investing, demystify jargon, and provide actionable steps for beginners.

Section 1: The Investment Landscape
What Is Investing?
Investing means putting your money to work with the goal of growing it over time. Think of it as planting seeds

today to reap a bountiful harvest in the future. Here are some key terms:

- Assets: Things you can invest in, such as stocks, bonds, real estate, or even your education.
- Returns: The profits or gains you make from your investments.
- Risk: The chance that your investment might lose value.

Investment Options

Stocks

- What Are Stocks? Stocks represent ownership in a company. When you buy shares, you become a shareholder.
- Why Invest in Stocks? Stocks historically offer higher returns than other assets, but they can be volatile.
- How to Get Started? Open a brokerage account, research companies, and consider index funds.

Bonds

- What Are Bonds? Bonds are loans you give to governments or corporations. In return, you receive interest payments.
- Why Invest in Bonds? Bonds are more stable than stocks and provide regular income.

- How to Get Started? Look into government bonds or corporate bonds.

Mutual Funds and ETFs

- What Are Mutual Funds and ETFs? These are investment vehicles that pool money from multiple investors to buy a diversified portfolio of stocks or bonds.
- Why Invest in Them? They offer diversification without requiring you to pick individual stocks.
- How to Get Started? Research low-cost index funds or ETFs.

Real Estate

- What Is Real Estate Investing? It involves buying property (like a house, apartment, or commercial space) to generate rental income or capital appreciation.
- Why Invest in Real Estate? Real estate can provide steady income and potential long-term growth.
- How to Get Started? Learn about real estate markets and consider real estate investment trusts (REITs).

Section 2: Getting Started
Setting Financial Goals

Before you invest, define your goals:

- Short-Term Goals: Saving for a vacation, emergency fund, or buying a car.
- Long-Term Goals: Retirement, buying a home, or funding your children's education.

Investing in Yourself

Self-Care

- Prioritize your mental and physical health. It's an investment in your overall well-being.
- Manage stress, exercise, eat well, and get enough rest.

Time Management

- Time is your most valuable resource. Invest it wisely.
- Learn time management techniques to balance work, study, and personal life.

Education

- Continuously learn and develop new skills.
- Consider certifications, workshops, or online courses.

Investing in Relationships

Social Connections

- Strong relationships reduce stress and improve mental health.

- Nurture friendships, join clubs, and attend social events.

Self-Reflection

- Evaluate your relationship with yourself. Be kind and supportive.
- Practice self-compassion and self-awareness.

Healthy Boundaries

- Maintain independence while nurturing connections.
- Set boundaries to protect your well-being.

Conclusion

Investing isn't just about money; it's about creating a fulfilling life. Start small, stay informed, and remember that every step counts. Whether you're investing in stocks or investing time in self-improvement, you're building a brighter future.

Feel free to explore further, ask questions, and take action. Your financial journey begins now!

CHAPTER 13: INSURANCE INFORMATION

Introduction
As a young adult, navigating the world of insurance can feel like deciphering a complex puzzle. Fear not! In this chapter, we'll unravel the mysteries of insurance by weaving in relatable stories and practical advice. Let's explore how insurance shields you from life's unexpected twists and turns.

Section 1: The Importance of Asset Protection
Why Protect Your Assets?
Meet Sarah, a recent college graduate. She landed her dream job and moved into a cozy apartment. Life was good until a reckless driver totaled her car. Without auto insur-

ance, Sarah faced a hefty repair bill and no transportation. Asset protection matters because:

- Lawsuits: Imagine being sued for an accident. Without liability coverage, your savings and assets are vulnerable.
- Financial Security: Insurance provides a safety net, ensuring you bounce back after setbacks.
- Risk Management: Identifying risks early prevents financial disasters.

Section 2: Types of Insurance
Auto Insurance: Sarah's Story

Sarah's car accident taught her the value of auto insurance. She had comprehensive coverage, which paid for repairs and medical bills. Without it, she'd be hitchhiking to work!

- Coverage: Auto insurance protects your vehicle, passengers, and other drivers.
- Benefits: Peace of mind, legal compliance, and financial support during accidents.

Homeowners or Renters Insurance: Alex's Tale

Alex rented a trendy loft. One day, a burst pipe flooded his place, ruining furniture and electronics. Luckily, he had renters insurance:

- Coverage: It safeguards personal belongings, liability, and additional living expenses.
- Benefits: Replacing stolen items, covering hotel costs during repairs, and avoiding legal hassles.

Health Insurance: Emma's Journey

Emma, a freelance artist, fell ill unexpectedly. Health insurance saved her from drowning in medical bills:

- Coverage: Pays for doctor visits, prescriptions, surgeries, and preventive care.
- Benefits: Access to quality healthcare without draining your savings.

Life Insurance: Mark's Legacy

Mark, a young father, purchased life insurance. Tragically, he passed away. His family received a lump sum:

- Coverage: Provides for loved ones after your death.
- Benefits: Funeral expenses, mortgage payments, and financial stability for survivors.

Umbrella Insurance: The Smiths' Shield

The Smiths hosted a pool party. A guest slipped, broke an arm, and sued. Their homeowners insurance maxed out, but umbrella insurance stepped in:

- Coverage: Extends liability protection beyond other policies.

- Benefits: Avoiding personal bankruptcy due to lawsuits.

Section 3: Risk Assessment
Identifying Risks: Jake's Dilemma
Jake started a small business. He assessed risks:

- Health Risks: What if he fell sick and couldn't work?
- Property Risks: Fire, theft, or natural disasters endanger his assets.
- Liability Risks: Customers suing him for faulty products.

Balancing Coverage and Affordability: Lisa's Lesson
Lisa researched insurance options:

- Assess Your Needs: She chose coverage based on her lifestyle and risks.
- Compare Quotes: Lisa found affordable policies without compromising protection.
- Budget Wisely: She allocated funds for premiums.

Section 4: Additional Asset
Protection Strategies Legal Tools: Maria's Shield
Maria set up a Domestic Asset Protection Trust (DAPT). It shielded her assets from creditors:

- Benefits: Legal protection, privacy, and peace of mind.

- Consequences Without It: Creditors seizing her savings.

Active Financial Management: Tom's Tactics

Tom maintained good records, built an emergency fund, and diversified investments:

- Benefits: Preparedness for emergencies and reduced financial risk.
- Consequences Without It: Chaos during crises and missed opportunities.

Conclusion

Remember, insurance isn't just paperwork—it's your safety net. Whether you're protecting your car, health, or dreams, make informed choices. Your financial story deserves a happy ending! ◈

Feel free to explore further resources and consult experts for personalized guidance!

CHAPTER 14: TAKING THE FIRST STEP

With the wealth of information provided in the previous chapters, it's natural to feel overwhelmed and unsure of where to start. However, the key is to begin somewhere that makes sense for you and adjust as needed. In this chapter, we'll explore how to take that first step, ask for help when needed, and lean on family and friends for support and advice.

Starting Small

Don't try to tackle everything at once. Start with one area that resonates with you, such as:
- Creating a budget
- Building an emergency fund

- Paying off debt
- Investing in your future

Break down larger goals into smaller, manageable tasks. Celebrate your successes and adjust your approach as needed.

Seeking Help

Don't be afraid to ask for help when you need it. Consider:

- Financial advisors or planners
- Credit counselors
- Online resources and forums
- Family and friends with financial expertise

Remember, asking for help is a sign of strength, not weakness.

Support System

Surround yourself with a supportive network of family and friends. They can offer:

- Emotional support and encouragement
- Practical advice and guidance
- Accountability and motivation

Don't be afraid to lean on them when you need it.

Adjusting Your Approach

As you progress on your financial journey, be willing to adjust your approach as needed. Life is unpredictable, and your financial plan should be flexible enough to accommodate changes.

- Regularly review and assess your progress
- Make adjustments to your budget, investments, or debt repayment plan

- Stay informed and educated on personal finance topics

Overcoming Obstacles

You will encounter obstacles on your financial journey. Don't let them discourage you. Instead:

- Identify the obstacle and its root cause
- Seek help and advice from your support system
- Adjust your approach and find a new solution

Staying Motivated

Staying motivated is crucial to achieving your financial goals. Celebrate your successes, no matter how small, and remind yourself why you started this journey in the first place.

- Set reminders and milestones to track your progress
- Share your goals with your support system to increase accountability
- Reward yourself for reaching milestones

Avoiding Common Pitfalls

As you work towards your financial goals, be aware of common pitfalls that can derail your progress.

- Lifestyle inflation: Avoid increasing spending as income rises
- Impulse purchases: Create a 30-day waiting period for non-essential buys
- Lack of emergency fund: Aim for 3-6 months' expenses in savings

Maintaining Momentum

Maintaining momentum is key to achieving your financial goals.

- Regularly review and adjust your budget

- Stay informed about personal finance and investing
- Continuously educate yourself on new strategies and techniques

Long-term Thinking

Remember, financial stability and security are long-term goals.

- Avoid getting caught up in get-rich-quick schemes
- Focus on steady, consistent progress
- Celebrate small victories along the way

Supporting Others

As you achieve your financial goals, consider supporting others in their financial journey.

- Share your knowledge and experience with friends and family
- Offer support and encouragement to those struggling financially
- Participate in online communities or forums to help others

Conclusion

Taking the first step towards financial stability and security can seem daunting, but it doesn't have to be. By starting small, seeking help when needed, and leaning on a supportive network, you can set yourself up for success. Remember to be patient, stay informed, and adjust your approach as needed. With time and effort, you'll be well on your way to achieving your financial goals.

Summary

A Tool for Navigating Adulthood

This book is designed to be a tool for navigating adulthood. It is not meant to be read cover to cover in one sitting, although you certainly can if you wish. Instead, it is structured in a way that allows you to pick and choose the chapters that are most relevant to you at any given time. Whether you are looking for advice on opening a bank account, managing multiple jobs, or saving for a vacation, you can find the information you need when you need it.

Each chapter is filled with practical tips, real-life examples, and actionable advice. I have drawn from my own experiences, as well as the experiences of others, to provide a comprehensive guide that covers a wide range of topics. My goal is to make this book a valuable resource that you can turn to whenever you face a new challenge or need guidance on a particular issue.

This book provides a structured approach to tackling the complexities of adulthood, with each chapter dedicated to a key aspect of living independently in a challenging economic environment. From the basics of financial literacy to the nuances of credit scores and investments, the book aims to equip young adults with the knowledge and skills necessary to thrive. Practical advice, real-world examples, and actionable steps will guide readers through the process of building a solid foundation for their adult lives. The fi-

CHAPTER 14: TAKING THE FIRST STEP

nal chapter looks to the future, encouraging continuous learning and adaptation in an ever-changing world.

www.ingramcontent.com/pod-product-compliance
Lightning Source LLC
LaVergne TN
LVHW012025060526
838201LV00061B/4470